Little Linguists' Library

Book Two: Je ne veux pas aller à l'école !

Written by William Collier
Illustrated by Adit Galih

Little Linguists' Library - Book Two: Je ne veux pas aller à l'école !
Copyright © 2020 by William Collier All rights reserved.
First Edition: 2020

Paperback ISBN: 978-1-9164703-6-1
Hardcover ISBN: 978-1-9164703-7-8

Written by William Collier
Illustrated by Adit Galih

No part of this book may be reproduced, scanned, or distributed in any printed or electronic form without permission. Please do not participate in or encourage piracy of copyrighted materials in violation of the author's rights. Thank you for respecting the hard work of this author.

This is a work of fiction. Names, characters, places, and incidents either are the product of the author's imagination or are used fictitiously, and any resemblance to locales, events, business establishments, or actual persons—living or dead—is entirely coincidental.

For Ruth, the newest little linguist.

DON'T FORGET TO DOWNLOAD YOUR FREE AUDIOBOOK!

Go to http://littlelinguistslibrary.com/how-to-use-the-books/

Your download code is:
littlelinguistsrock03

Thank you for choosing Little Linguists' Library®. We're very excited to have you here and to accompany you as you start your journey as a language-learning family.

Chez Pierre...

Chez Claire...

1. Zhuh nuh vuh pa ah-lay ah leh-col.

2. Zhuh nuh vuh pa ah-lay ah leh-col.

1. Say luh prom-mee-yay zhoor.
   Leh-col ay tam-moo-zont.

2. Say luh prom-mee-yay zhoor.
   Leh-col ay for-mee-da-bluh.

1. Tee-yahn. Say tah proff. Oh-re-vwah, Puh-tee Pee-air.
2. Bohn-zhoor. Zhuh ma-pell Ma-dam Soh-lay.
3. Tee-yahn. Say tah proff. Oh-re-vwah, Clare.

1. Ass-see-yay twah lah, Clare.

1. Zhuh nuh con-nay pehr-sonne.

1. Zhuh tuh con-nay, Puh-tee Pee-air.

2. Oo-wee, Clare. Zhuh tuh con-nay oh-see.

1. Bohn-zhoor. Zhuh ma-pell Ma-dam Soh-lay.
2. Bohn-zhoor, ma-dam. Zhuh ma-pell Sah-rah.

1. Ass-see-yay twah lah, Sah-rah.

1. Bohn-zhoor. Zhuh ma-pell Clare ay eel sah-pell Pee-air.

2. Bohn-zhoor.

3. Bohn-zhoor.

1. Man-tuh-nohn ohn vah ay-too-dee-ay lay nom-bruh.

1. Zhaim lay nom-bruh.

2. Zhuh naim pa lay nom-bruh.

1. Uhn, duh, twah.

Plus tard...

1. Man-tuh-nohn say lur duh day-zhuh-nay.

1. Zha-dor lay pom.

2. Zha-dor lay sonne-dweesh oh froh-maazh.

3. Zha-dor lay bah-nan.

1. Voo-zet cohm-bee-ahn dohn la fah-mee ?

2. Noo somme cah-truh - mwah, ma mair, ma sur ay mohn frair.

1. Voo-zet cohm-bee-ahn dohn la fah-mee ?

2. Noo somme sank - mwah, ma mair, mohn pair, mohn frair ay ma sur.

1. Man-tuh-nohn, lay zon-fon, say lur doo cont.

2. Zhaim lay cont.

3. Mwah oh-see

4. Lay cont son tam-moo-zohn.

1. Say la fahn duh la zhoor-nay.

2. Zha-dor leh-col.

1. Oh re-vwah, too luh mond.

2. Oh re-vwah, Ma-dam Soh-lay.

1. Set-tay coh-mohn ?

2. For-mee-da-bluh.
   Leh-col ay tam-moo-zont.

1. Kess kuh voo za-vay fay ?

2. Zhay ay-too-dee-yay lay nom-bruh.

3. Zhay ay-coo-tay uhn cont.

4. Zhay zhoo-ay.

1. Kess keel-ee-ya ?

2. Zhuh nuh vuh pa ah-lay ah la may-zohn !

GLOSSARY

Translations

Page 1

<u>Surtitre (Surtitle)</u>: Chez Pierre / Chez Claire — At Peter's / Claire's house

<u>Petit Pierre / Claire Courage</u>: Je ne veux pas aller à l'école. — I don't want to go to school.

Page 2

<u>M. Petit</u>: C'est le premier jour. L'école est amusante. — It's the first day. School is fun.

<u>Mme. Courage</u>: C'est le premier jour. L'école est formidable. — It's the first day. School is fantastic.

Page 3

<u>M. Petit</u>: Tiens. C'est ta prof. Au revoir, Petit Pierre. — Look. It's your teacher. Goodbye, Little Peter.

<u>Mme. Courage</u>: Tiens. C'est ta prof. Au revoir, Claire. — Look. It's your teacher. Goodbye, Claire.

<u>Mme. Soleil</u>: Bonjour ! Je m'appelle Madame Soleil. — Hello! My name is Mrs Sun..

Page 4

<u>Mme. Soleil</u>: Assieds-toi là, Claire. — Sit there, Claire..

Claire Courage: Je ne connais personne.

Petit Pierre: Je ne connais personne.

Claire Courage: Je te connais, Petit Pierre !

Petit Pierre: Oui, Claire. Je te connais aussi.

Mme. Soleil: Bonjour ! Je m'appelle Madame Soleil.

Sarah: Bonjour, madame. Je m'appelle Sarah.

Mme. Soleil: Assieds-toi là, Sarah.

Sarah: Bonjour.

Claire Courage: Bonjour ! Je m'appelle Claire et il s'appelle Pierre.

Petit Pierre: Bonjour.

Page 5

I don't know anyone.

I don't know anyone.

Page 6

I know you, Little Peter!

Yes, Claire. I know you too.

Page 7

Hello! My name is Mrs Sun.

Hello, miss. My name is Sarah.

Page 8

Sit there, Sarah..

Page 9

Hello.

Hello! My name is Claire and his name is Peter.

Hello.

Page 10

Mme. Soleil: Maintenant on va étudier les nombres.

Now we're going to study numbers.

Page 11

Claire Courage: J'aime les nombres.

I like numbers.

Petit Pierre: Je n'aime pas les nombres.

I don't like numbers.

Page 12

Mme. Soleil: Un, deux, trois.

One, two, three.

Claire Courage, Petit Pierre, Sarah: Un, deux, trois.

One, two, three.

Page 13

Surtitre (Surtitle): Plus tard

Later

Mme. Soleil: Maintenant c'est l'heure de déjeuner.

Now it's lunch time.

Page 14

Claire Courage: J'adore les pommes.

I love apples.

Sarah: J'adore les sandwichs au fromage.

I love cheese sandwiches.

Petit Pierre: J'adore les bananes.

I love bananas.

Page 15

<u>Claire Courage</u>: Vous êtes combien dans la famille ?

How many people are there in your family?

<u>Sarah</u>: Nous sommes quatre - moi, ma mère, ma sœur et mon frère.

There's four of us - me, my mother, my sister and my brother.

Page 16

<u>Sarah</u>: Vous êtes combien dans la famille ?

How many people are there in your family?

<u>Claire Courage</u>: Nous sommes cinq - moi, ma mère, mon père, mon frère et ma sœur.

There's five of us - me, my mum, my dad, my brother and my sister.

Page 17

<u>Surtitre (Surtitle)</u>: Après le déjeuner

After lunch

<u>Mme. Soleil</u>: Maintenant, les enfants, c'est l'heure du conte.

Now, children, it's story time.

<u>Claire Courage</u>: J'aime les contes.

I like stories.

<u>Petit Pierre</u>: Moi aussi.

Me too.

<u>Sarah</u>: Les contes sont amusants.

Stories are fun.

Page 18

<u>Surtitre (Surtitle)</u>: Plus tard

Later

<u>Mme. Soleil</u>: C'est la fin de la journée.

It's the end of the day.

<u>Claire Courage, Petit Pierre, Sarah</u>: J'adore l'école.

I love school.

Page 19

<u>Mme. Soleil</u>: Au revoir, tout le monde.   Goodbye, everybody.

<u>Claire Courage, Petit Pierre, Sarah</u>: Au revoir, Madame Soleil.   Goodbye, Mrs Sun.

Page 20

<u>M. Petit</u>: C'était comment ?   How was it?

<u>Claire Courage, Petit Pierre, Sarah</u>: Formidable ! L'école est amusante.   Brilliant! School is fun.

Page 21

<u>La maman de Sarah</u>: Qu'est-ce que vous avez fait ?   What did you do?

<u>Claire Courage</u>: J'ai étudié les nombres.   I studied numbers.

<u>Sarah</u>: J'ai écouté un conte.   I listened to a story.

<u>Petit Pierre</u>: J'ai joué.   I played.

Page 22

<u>M. Courage</u>: Qu'est-ce qu'il y a ?   What's wrong?

<u>Claire Courage, Petit Pierre, Sarah</u>: Je ne veux pas aller à la maison !   I don't want to go home!

ACKNOWLEDGEMENTS

Thank you to everyone who has supported the production of Book Two of Little Linguists' Library.

Particular thanks go to:

My wife.

My parents.

Our fantastic voice actors, Katia Filipović and Roger Maréchal. Check out your free audiobook download to hear them (see details at front of book).

www.ingramcontent.com/pod-product-compliance
Lightning Source LLC
LaVergne TN
LVHW070535120526
838202LV00119B/2620